The 90-DAY

Happiness

Journal

The scientific solution for a life of happiness

by

Prof. Dr. Detlef Beeker

Prof. Dr. Detlef Beeker

Happiness Researcher

The 90-Day Happiness Journal Copyright © 2019
by Prof. Dr. Detlef Beeker

Happiness research loves diaries.

Our true purpose is to be happy.
- Dalai Lama

You want to be happier? It's not a bad idea because happy people are not only happier, but they are also healthier and more successful.

This journal is a particularly effortless way to become happier. You don't have to meditate, exercise or do psychotherapy; no, you just have to answer three questions a day for a few minutes. This automatically changes your perspective and perception. Suddenly little things like a rosy sunset or a ladybug on top of a blade of grass will make you happy.

Why this diary makes you happy

The special thing about this journal is that it will really make you happier. How do I know? Because all the questions you find in this diary have been scientifically researched and found to lead to greater happiness. The entire journal is based on the findings of happiness research. Every single question you are asked has been tested in studies. In the chapter "The questions in detail", I have presented the scientific evidence. You can also find out the effect for yourself by testing your happiness before and after the 90 days. You will learn how to do this in the next section, "How happy are you?"

Why gratitude journals don't work (by the way: this is not a gratitude journal)

"Whoo! Really?" I hear the reader exclaim in disbelief. "There are so many gratitude diaries. They're all worthless?" My answer is an unequivocal: "Yes!"

Let me explain: Gratitude journals are designed for the reader to write down a few things every day for which he is grateful. Scientists have found that it doesn't work. At the latest, after a few days we start to fill in the diary mechanically. This is understandable because if I have to list three things every day for which I am grateful, it will be difficult and mechanical. The problem: If it becomes mechanical, then it has no effect. We have to feel a little bit of gratitude in order for the diary to have a positive effect. Happiness researchers have found through studies that it is best to keep a gratitude diary only once a week. This is a counterintuitive result because we usually think: "The more, the better." This does not apply to gratitude.

Let the well-known happiness researcher Prof. Sonja Lyubomirsky have her say. She conducted a study in which the participants were divided into three groups: One group kept a gratitude diary only once a week on Sunday evenings. The next group practiced gratitude three times a week, and the control group did no practice.

"In comparison to a control group (i.e. people who did not practice any kind of practice), the gratitude group reported a much stronger increase in their state of happiness from before to after the intervention. Interestingly, this effect was only observed in those who showed gratitude every Sunday evening. The participants, who counted their blessings three times a week could not benefit from this."

The subjects who practiced gratitude three times a week could not achieve any effect. This is strong stuff. This book takes this important insight into account: You will practice gratitude only once a week.

How to use this journal

- **A glimpse of good feelings**: One thing is important: The questions should not be answered mechanically. If possible, you should put yourself in the situation. For example, consider the question "What was beautiful or pleasant today?" that is asked in the diary. When you come across this question, briefly relive the situation. The question "why" helps you. To become happy, it is good if you at least feel a subtle positive feeling. But even more important is that you don't stress yourself out. Especially at the beginning, it's possible that you simply don't feel anything. That doesn't matter at all. The questions have an effect anyway. You will recognize this, for example, when you suddenly pause during the day and think: "Ah, that was a beautiful moment right now. I will write it in my journal tonight!"

- **Answer the questions freely:** If, for example, you answer the question of what was pleasant today with "The cheese roll tasted so delicious," then that is completely ok. You are the boss, and you decide what you write. Sometimes the inner critic says: "No, you can't write that! You thought it was nice to eat a cheese roll? That's pathetic!" Don't let that mislead you. Every answer is right.

- **You should fill out the diary in the evening:** This is mainly due to question #1: "What went well today?" In addition to this, the evening is a good time; we are quiet, and the work of the day is done. We can take the good feelings of diary keeping with us to sleep.

- **What to do if you are not in the mood:** Don't stress! Of course it would be great if you consistently keep the diary, but sometimes you just don't feel like it. For such days I suggest that you just make up your mind to write a little. Question #1 is: "What was pleasant or beautiful today? Why? Name 3 things." Just write down a situation. It only takes a minute. If you are still motivated, write down the other things as well. Are you still there? Then write something to question #2 and then to question #3. That should be the order. Question #1 is most important. By doing a bit every day, journaling becomes a habit. Then you automatically do it and don't have to think about it anymore.

How happy are you?

Happiness researchers believe that people themselves know best whether they are happy. Therefore, the most common way to measure happiness is to simply ask. Science is sometimes not that complicated. What does such a survey look like? There are different variants. Many happiness researchers only ask about life satisfaction - this is sufficient for a large number of studies.

In the following pages you will see a more detailed variant in which you are asked four questions. It was developed by the happiness researcher Sonja Lyubomirsky. Don't think too long; answer the questions from your gut:

1. In general, I consider myself...

1	2	3	4	5	6	7

not a very
happy person

a very
happy person

2. Compared with the most of my peers, I consider myself...

1	2	3	4	5	6	7

less happy

more happy

3. Some people are generally very happy. They enjoy life

regardless of what is going on, getting the most out of everything. To what extent does this characterization describe you?

1	2	3	4	5	6	7

not at all   a great deal

4. Some people are generally not very happy. Although they are not depressed, they never seem as happy as they might be. To what extent does this characterization describe you?

1	2	3	4	5	6	7

a great deal   not at all

Make a circle around the value that applies to you. Then calculate your average value. The resulting value is your current happiness level.

For example, Felix, a friend of mine, circled 6 in question 1, 5 in question 2, 6 in question 3, and 5 in the last question. He summed up his values and divided them by the number of questions to get the average value: (6+5+6+5)/4 = 5.5, so Felix has a happiness level of 5.5.

On average, people achieve between 4.5 and 5.5. Students achieve fewer happiness points on average, slightly less than 5. Working Adults and pensioners achieve slightly more. They are on average 5.6. If, for example, you are a student and are over 5, then you have above average happiness. By the way, whatever your result, this diary will improve your level of happiness.

I would be happy if you could answer the above questions and find out your happiness level. Why? I want to prove to you that this diary actually makes you happier. After the 90 days, another happiness test is waiting for you. If scientific curiosity grabs you, you can also determine your happiness level every 30 days. You will see that your happiness increases.

The questions in detail

This chapter is quite long and slightly technical. If you have some spare time at the moment, please read it. It represents the scientific foundation of the individual questions. In addition, the questions are explained in detail with examples. This means that if you are not quite sure how to answer a question, you can look it up in this chapter. But if you'd rather start writing your journal now, skip this chapter. You'll still have time to read it later.

Every day you'll be asked three questions. All questions are based on modern happiness research. The questions are repeated every week. This means that every week is the same, but the individual days are different. For example, the questions of Day 1 are the same as those of Day 8. Therefore only the first seven days will be discussed below.

Question #1

One of the central techniques in happiness research is the Three Good Things. This is a great technique that guarantees an increase in happiness. It is easy to practice and immediately creates good feelings. That's why this is the basic technique of this journal.

What do the scientists say? The positive review of the day has proven to be a very successful technique. Depression eases, and happiness increases. Up to six months after the participants of a study applied the Three Good Things, the positive effects were still measurable. Even in severely depressed subjects, some of whom were unable to get out of bed, this technique was surprisingly effective. After only two weeks the condition improved significantly in 94% of the participants. The good thing is that you can use this technique every day.

Three Good Things is about finding three events and writing them down. You can deepen the experience by asking "why are these things good?"

In the Three Good Things there are three variants, namely "pleasant experiences," "use of your strengths," and "meaningful experiences." You will get to know all three variants in this diary.

1. Pleasant experiences: This question is asked on days 1, 3, 5 and 6. It says: **"What went well today?"**

Find three pleasant experiences. Of course you can write more at any time, but three things are enough. You can deepen the experience by asking: **"Why was that pleasant?"** Here are a few examples:

Question: "What went well today?" Answer: "I played with my son this morning." Question: "Why?" Answer: "It was so sweet to cuddle with him; he laughed so much, and his sweet eyes lit up."

Question: "What went well today?" Answer: "I rode my bike today. That was fun." Question: "Why?" Answer: "Actually I wanted to watch a TV series. But I got my act together after all. It was nice because it was a good feeling to move. I also drove through a beautiful forest, which was good."

The "why?" question deepens the experience. You can answer the "why" question freely -- you can't do anything wrong.

2: Use your strengths: You will meet this question on days 2 and 4, where you will reflect on three occasions today where you have used your strengths. Ask yourself: **"Where have I used my strengths today?"** You can deepen this by then asking the question: **"Why?"** Here are a few examples:

Question: "Where have I used my strengths today? Answer: "I played with my little son this morning". Question: "Why? Answer: "I am a loving father and can play well with the little one".

Question: "Where have I used my strengths today?"

Answer: "I rode my bike today. It was fun." Question: "Why?" Answer: "I'm disciplined, and although I was tired, I still rode a bike."

3. Meaningful experiences: You will be asked this question on day 7. At the end of the day you write down three meaningful experiences you had today. Ask yourself the question: "**What was meaningful today?**" And then: "**Why**?" Here are a few examples:

Question: "What was meaningful today?" Answer: "I played with my son this morning." Question: "Why?" Answer: "My son gives meaning to my life."

Question: "What was meaningful today?" Answer: "Today the sunset was so beautiful." Question: "Why?" Answer: "It was a meaningful experience because it showed me how beautiful the world is and that there is more than everyday life."

If you have less time, just answer question #1. It will give you good feelings in the short and long term.

Question #2

Question #2 uses different techniques of happiness research.

Day 1

Day 1 is about a very important feeling: gratitude. Studies have shown the many positive effects. People who are grateful are happier, more energetic, more optimistic, and more likely to feel positive feelings. Furthermore, grateful people are more helpful, sympathetic, forgiving, spiritual and religious, and less materialistic than people who are less grateful. Grateful people suffer less often from depression, nervousness, loneliness, envy, and neuroses. These are many advantages. Let's look at two studies from happiness research as examples:

In the first study on gratitude of this kind, the participants were asked to write down things they were grateful for once a week for ten weeks. The control group, on the other hand, should write down five annoyances a day. A comparison was made after ten weeks, and the results were amazing. The gratitude group was more optimistic and happy with their lives compared to the control group. Even their health had improved; there were fewer physical symptoms like headaches, coughing, etc. And on top of that, they did more physical activity. An amazing result, don't you think? The participants did this exercise only once a week. That's not much, but it had strong effects.

Another study was done by Park, Peterson, and Seligman. They investigated to what extent 24 character strengths influence our life satisfaction. Gratitude is one of the most important factors. Gratitude determines 20% of our life satisfaction. This is an enormous amount. Therefore, if you are not grateful, your life satisfaction is 20% lower than if you are grateful.

How do we become grateful? How can we train gratitude? A very good way is to keep a gratitude diary. You write down up to five things for which you are grateful. Studies have shown that this exercise is most effective when done only once a week. Many self-help guides recommend practicing this exercise daily. Why should once a week be better? It is important that this exercise is not done mechanically. Gratitude should be felt. This works best if you do it once a week.

Goal: Cultivate gratitude

Action plan: Write down three to five things you're grateful for. It is important that you feel a sense of gratitude -- at least a little. Feel the feeling. Mechanical writing has no effect.

Tip: It doesn't matter what you're thankful for. Whether you're thankful for your marriage, that your bike is working again or that this annoying pimple has finally disappeared, there are no limits to your imagination. The main thing is that you are actually grateful for it.

Day 2

On day 2 your optimism will be trained with the exercise "Best Possible Self." Studies have shown that this technique is very effective. Just imagining the best possible future releases positive emotions. At the same time it can give your life a direction, because you realize that this goal, this vision, is actually achievable.

The first study of this kind was conducted by Laura King, a professor from Missouri. For four consecutive days, the participants had to write down for 20 minutes how they imagined their best possible future self. Compared to the control group, the participants had a significant increase in well-being immediately after the exercise. A few weeks later, they felt happier and in the coming months they suffered less from physical illness.[1]

Goal:

- **Training your optimism muscle**: You get used to looking positively into the future.

- **Visualization of your best possible self**: You form a vision for your life.

- **Technique**: Take 20 - 30 minutes. Imagine how your life looks best after one, five, and ten years. You worked hard, and everything went well. Imagine that you have realized all your life dreams. Write everything down.

---

[1] King (2001): "The health benefits of writing about life goals." *Personality and Social Psychology Bulletin*, 27: 798–807.

- Remember, everything is going well. If your inner critic comes forward and doubts, then look for solutions and continue to look positively into the future.

Tips:

- Sometimes there is a lack of motivation. Then just make up your mind to write a sentence. So just fill in one line in your diary -- that's enough. If more is written once you get started, all the better!

- Think big! Don't let concerns guide you but see what you really want. We are used to thinking of the obstacles: "Oh, I can't do that anyway! That's far too difficult!" We are used to thinking small. We don't dare to do great things. These are only beliefs. Why shouldn't you be able to achieve great things? There are countless examples of people who have achieved great things. You can do it too. So don't set your goals too small. Dream big! Nevertheless, your vision should be realistic. It should be possible.

- Everything turned out best: You imagine, for example, that you have set up your own business, and your business is going great.

- Training our optimism muscle: This expression comes from Sonja Lyubomirsky. We are used to looking negatively into the future. With this exercise, we train our optimism and create lasting good feelings.

- Side effect - life dreams: As a side effect of this exercise, you get to know your true life dreams. Having life dreams is motivating. You can decide to make these dreams come true. But you don't have to. The exercise itself is only about the imagination, not the implementation.

- **Write down doubts**: It is completely normal for doubts to arise. Deal with them. Concerns can sometimes be justified and then it is good if you find solutions. Often doubts are not justified. Then it is good to know them and make it clear that they have no basis.

Day 3 und 6

Days 3 and 6 are about the feeling of joy. To train this, we use techniques from Positive Journaling. This is a new development from positive psychology. In Positive Journaling, feelings such as joy, serenity or reverence are intentionally cultivated through diary writing. A large-scale study could prove many positive effects.

> *"I was thrilled with the results of the study. They showed that Positive Jour-naling seemed to be a valuable way to discover, generate and reflect our posi-tive emotions. This way of writing could help us cultivate our great emotions and use these emotions to move on our individual paths to self growth."*[2]

This quotation comes from one of those responsible for the

---

[2] Megan C. Hayes and Kate Hefferon: "Not like rose-tinted glasses... like taking a pair of dirty glasses off: A pilot inter-vention using positive emotions in expressive writing:" International Journal of Wellbeing 5, no. 4, (December 2015): 78–95.

study, Megan C. Hayes.

On **day 3**, the diary asks you the following question:

Question #2: Write about an event in the past that brought you joy. What happened? Where have you been? What exactly did you feel?

You are completely free with the answer; it can be a small thing. Maybe you enjoyed a sunset yesterday or a delicious ice cream. Maybe it was your first kiss or the birth of your child. Everything is allowed, as long as you felt joy. It doesn't have to have been ecstatic joy -- no, a small, subtle one is quite enough.

The question on **day 6** is:

Question #2: How could you give yourself a little joy every day? Find ideas.

For both questions, it is important that you feel a little bit of this joy. If this is difficult, dive deeper into the experience by asking: "What did I see, what did I hear, feel, and smell?"

Days 4 and 7

"Laughter is healthy." Everyone knows this saying, and it's true.

Studies have shown many positive effects of laughter. The body releases a cocktail of mood-enhancing hormones. At the same time, blood flow is increased by 50%. That is enormous. Laughing even burns calories. If you laugh 15 minutes a day, you lose five pounds a year. By the way, our brain is not able to distinguish between real and artificial laughter.

In the journal you will find the exercise Three Funny Things. It is a great and scientifically proven way to bring laughter and happiness into your life:

In one study, the participants practiced Three Funny Things

every evening every day for a week. The results were very positive. Immediately after the exercise, depression decreased. A gain in happiness could even be observed six months later, compared to a control group reporting on their early memories.[3]

Goal: Happiness and laughter

Action plan: The diary asks you the question:

What was funny today? Why? Name three things.

They don't have to be laughing fits. If you smiled at an event, that's enough. Write it down! As with any exercise, it is good if you experience the feeling a little. The question "Why?" will help you. It deepens the experience.

Day 5

There's an unusual exercise on day five. This is about re-evaluating seemingly negative events and finding the positive. Life is not always sunshine. Often we are shaken by negative events. It can be big things like losing your job or small things like a rainy day. The ability to reframe them, to reinterpret them positively, is important. This has been scientifically confirmed:

Participants in a study who completed this exercise daily for three weeks reported at the end of the study a greater commitment to life and less dysfunctional thinking (e.g. the belief that small failures lead a person to failure) than at the beginning of the study. Participants who were prone to pessimism profited particularly from the exercise and showed fewer depressive symptoms afterwards. However, these effects seemed to subside two months later, indicating

---

[3] Wellenzohn, S., Proyer, R. T., & Ruch, W. (2016): "Humor-based online positive psychology interventions: A randomized placebo-controlled long-term trial." Journal of Positive Psychology, 11(6), 584-94.

the need to repeat the practice regularly.[4]

Goal: Resilience

Action plan: The diary asks you the following question:

What didn't go the way you intended last week? Find the positive. What could be the lesson and the blessing?

So take a situation from last week and write down what can be positive about it. Which situation you pick is entirely up to you. Whatever comes to your mind will be the right thing to do.

The question *"What could be the lesson and blessing?"* helps you to reinterpret the situation positively.

Question #3

This question also comes from Positive Journaling. Like questions #2 of days 3 and 6, it cultivates the feeling of joy. It reads:

Question #3: What are you looking forward to tomorrow?

This question is a positive attunement for tomorrow. Write down something that comes to mind. It doesn't have to be great, a little thing like morning coffee is enough.

---

[4] Sergeant, S., & Mongrain, M. (2014): "An online optimism intervention reduces depression in pessimistic individuals." Journal of Consulting and Clinical Psychology, 82(2), 263-274.

Day 1

Date _____

> *Our true purpose is to be happy. — Dalai Lama*

Question #1: What went well today? Why? Find 3 pleasant experiences.

1. _____

_____

2. _____

_____

3. _____

_____

Question #2: Write down 3-5 things you're grateful for.

1. _____
2. _____
3. _____
4. _____
5. _____

Question #3: What are you looking forward to tomorrow?

_____

Day 2

Date _____

> *The man who removes a mountain starts by carrying away small stones. — William Faulkner*

Question #1: Where have I used my strengths today? Why? Name 3 things.

1.

2.

3.

Question #2: Imagine a future for yourself in which everything went as you imagined it would. You have given your best, worked hard, and achieved all your goals. Now write down what you imagine.

Day 3

Date _____

Question #1: What went well today? Why? Find 3 pleasant experiences.

1.

2.

3.

Question #2: Write about an event in the past that has given you joy. What happened? Where have you been? What exactly did you feel?

Question #3: What are you looking forward to tomorrow?

Day 4

Date _____

> *If the way is beautiful, let's not ask where it leads. — Anonymous*

Question #1: Where have I used my strengths today? Why? Name 3 things.

1.

_____

2.

_____

3.

_____

Question #2: What was funny today? Why? Name 3 things.

1.

_____

2.

_____

3.

_____

Question #3: What are you looking forward to tomorrow?

_____

Day 5

Date _____

> Happiness is not a gift from the gods, but the
> fruit of an inner mindset. — Erich Fromm

Question #1: What went well today? Why? Find 3 pleasant experiences.

1.

_____

_____

2.

_____

_____

3.

_____

_____

Question #2: What didn't go the way you intended last week? Find the positive. What could be the lesson and the blessing?

_____

_____

_____

_____

Question #3: What are you looking forward to tomorrow?

_____

Day 6

> *The happiness of the moment cannot be saved*
> *for later. — Ernst Ferstl*

Question #1: What went well today? Why? Find 3 pleasant experiences.

1. _____

   _____

2. _____

   _____

3. _____

   _____

Question #2: How could you give yourself a little joy every day? Find ideas.

_____

_____

_____

_____

_____

Question #3: What are you looking forward to tomorrow?

_____

Day 7

Date _____

Question #1: What was meaningful today? Why? Name three things.

1.

2.

3.

Question #2: What was funny today? Why? Name three things.

1.

2.

3.

Question #3: What are you looking forward to tomorrow?

Day 8

> *We strive more to avoid pain than to gain joy. –*
> *Sigmund Freud*

Question #1: What went well today? Why? Find 3
pleasant experiences.

1.

2.

3.

Question #2: Write down 3-5 things you're grateful for.

1.

2.

3.

4.

5.

Question #3: What are you looking forward to tomorrow?

Day 9

> *Even a journey of a thousand miles begins with the first step. – Laotse*

Question #1: Where have I used my strengths today? Why? Name 3 things.

1.

_____

2.

_____

3.

_____

_____

Question #2: Imagine a future for yourself in which everything went as you imagined it would. You have given your best, worked hard, and achieved all your goals. Now write down what you imagine.

_____

_____

_____

_____

_____

_____

Day 10

> *If you are not satisfied with what you have, you would not be satisfied with what you want.*
> *– Berthold Auerbach*

Question #1: What went well today? Why? Find 3 pleasant experiences.

1. _____

   _____

2. _____

   _____

3. _____

   _____

Question #2: Write about an event in the past that has given you joy. What happened? Where have you been? What exactly did you feel?

_____

_____

_____

_____

Question #3: What are you looking forward to tomorrow?

_____

Day 11

Date _____

> Whoever starts everything with a smile will suc-
> ceed most of all. – Dalai Lama

Question #1: Where have I used my strengths today? Why? Name 3 things.

1.

2.

3.

Question #2: What was funny today? Why? Name three things.

1.

2.

3.

Question #3: What are you looking forward to tomor-row?

Day 12

Date _____

> *Live as if you were dying tomorrow. Learn as if you live forever. – Mahatma Gandhi*

Question #1: What went well today? Why? Find 3 pleasant experiences.

1. _____
_____

2. _____
_____

3. _____
_____

Question #2: What didn't go the way you intended last week? Find the positive. What could be the lesson and the blessing?

_____

_____

_____

_____

Question #3: What are you looking forward to tomorrow?

_____

Day 13

Date _____

> *The joy is everywhere. It is only a matter of discovering it. – Confucius*

Question #1: What went well today? Why? Find 3 pleasant experiences.

1. _____
_____

2. _____
_____

3. _____
_____

Question #2: How could you give yourself a little joy every day? Find ideas.

_____
_____
_____
_____
_____

Question #3: What are you looking forward to tomorrow?

_____

Day 14

> You can't stop waves, but you can learn to surf.
> — Jon Kabat-Zinn

Question #1: What was meaningful today? Why? Name three things.

1.
_____

2.
_____

3.
_____

_____

Question #2: What was funny today? Why? Name three things.

1.
_____

2.
_____

3.
_____

Question #3: What are you looking forward to tomorrow?

_____

Day 15

Date _____

Question #1: What went well today? Why? Find 3 pleasant experiences.

1. _____

_____

2. _____

_____

3. _____

_____

Question #2: Write down 3-5 things you're grateful for.

1. _____
2. _____
3. _____
4. _____
5. _____

Question #3: What are you looking forward to tomorrow?

_____

Day 16

Date _____

Question #1: Where have I used my strengths today?
Why? Name 3 things.

1. _____

_____

2. _____

_____

3. _____

_____

Question #2: Imagine a future for yourself in which everything went as you imagined it would. You have given
your best, worked hard, and achieved all your goals.
Now write down what you imagine.

_____

_____

_____

_____

_____

_____

Day 17

Date _____

> *A sense of gratitude mixes with every high joy.*
> *— Marie von Ebner-Eschenbach*

Question #1: What went well today? Why? Find 3 pleasant experiences.

1. _____

_____

2. _____

_____

3. _____

_____

Question #2: Write about an event in the past that has given you joy. What happened? Where have you been? What exactly did you feel?

_____

_____

_____

_____

Question #3: What are you looking forward to tomorrow?

_____

Day 18

> *If you always follow all the rules, you*
> *miss all the fun.– Kathrin Hepburn*

Question #1: Where have I used my strengths today?
Why? Name 3 things.

1.

_____

2.

_____

3.

_____

_____

Question #2: What was funny today? Why? Name three
things.

1.

_____

2.

_____

3.

_____

Question #3: What are you looking forward to tomorrow?

_____

Day 19

Date _____

Question #1: What went well today? Why? Find 3
pleasant experiences.

1. _____

_____

2. _____

_____

3. _____

_____

Question #2: What didn't go the way you intended last
week? Find the positive. What could be the lesson and
the blessing?

_____

_____

_____

_____

_____

Question #3: What are you looking forward to tomorrow?

_____

Day 20

Date _____

Question #1: What went well today? Why? Find 3 pleasant experiences.

1. _____

   _____

2. _____

   _____

3. _____

   _____

   _____

Question #2: How could you give yourself a little joy every day? Find ideas.

_____

_____

_____

_____

_____

Question #3: What are you looking forward to tomorrow?

_____

Day 21

Date _____

Question #1: What was meaningful today? Why? Name
three things.

1.
_____

_____

2.
_____

_____

3.
_____

_____

Question #2: What was funny today? Why? Name three
things.

1.
_____

_____

2.
_____

_____

3.
_____

_____

Question #3: What are you looking forward to tomorrow?

_____

Day 22

Date _____

> *Gratitude is the feeling when the heart remembers. – Anonymous*

Question #1: What went well today? Why? Find 3 pleasant experiences.

1. _____

_____

2. _____

_____

3. _____

_____

Question #2: Write down 3-5 things you're grateful for.

1. _____
2. _____
3. _____
4. _____
5. _____

Question #3: What are you looking forward to tomorrow?

_____

Day 23

> *If everything seems to turn against you, remember that the plane takes off against the wind, not with it. - Henry Ford*

Question #1: Where have I used my strengths today? Why? Name 3 things.

1. _____

   _____

2. _____

   _____

3. _____

   _____

Question #2: Imagine a future for yourself in which everything went as you imagined it would. You have given your best, worked hard, and achieved all your goals. Now write down what you imagine.

_____

_____

_____

_____

_____

_____

Day 24

Date _____

> *The man who has no visions or dreams will never really achieve great things! – Nils Mewus*

Question #1: What went well today? Why? Find 3 pleasant experiences.

1.

_____

_____

2.

_____

_____

3.

_____

_____

Question #2: Write about an event in the past that has given you joy. What happened? Where have you been? What exactly did you feel?

_____

_____

_____

_____

Question #3: What are you looking forward to tomorrow?

_____

Day 25

Date _____

Question #1: Where have I used my strengths today? Why? Name 3 things.

1. _____

_____

2. _____

_____

3. _____

_____

Question #2: What was funny today? Why? Name three things.

1. _____

_____

2. _____

_____

3. _____

_____

Question #3: What are you looking forward to tomorrow?

_____

Day 26

> The only thing we lose when we accept challenges is our fear! – David Tatuljan

Question #1: What went well today? Why? Find 3 pleasant experiences.

1.

_____

2.

_____

3.

_____

_____

Question #2: What didn't go the way you intended last week? Find the positive. What could be the lesson and the blessing?

_____

_____

_____

_____

Question #3: What are you looking forward to tomorrow?

_____

Day 27

Date _____

> The most important thing is to enjoy your life -
> to be happy - that's all that matters.
> – Audrey Hepburn

Question #1: What went well today? Why? Find 3 pleasant experiences.

1.

2.

3.

Question #2: How could you give yourself a little joy every day? Find ideas.

Question #3: What are you looking forward to tomorrow?

Day 28

Date _____

> *Humor is the medicine that costs the least and*
> *is the easiest to take. – Giovanni Guareschi*

Question #1: What was meaningful today? Why? Name three things.

1.

_____

2.

_____

3.

_____

_____

Question #2: What was funny today? Why? Name three things.

1.

_____

2.

_____

3.

_____

Question #3: What are you looking forward to tomorrow?

_____

Day 29

Date _____

Question #1: What went well today? Why? Find 3 pleasant experiences.

1.
_____

_____

2.
_____

_____

3.
_____

_____

Question #2: Write down 3-5 things you're grateful for.

1.
_____
2.
_____
3.
_____
4.
_____
5.
_____

Question #3: What are you looking forward to tomor-row?

_____

Day 30

Date _____

Question #1: Where have I used my strengths today? Why? Name 3 things.

1.
_____

_____

2.
_____

_____

3.
_____

_____

Question #2: Imagine a future for yourself in which everything went as you imagined it would. You have given your best, worked hard, and achieved all your goals. Now write down what you imagine.

_____

_____

_____

_____

_____

_____

Day 31

Date _____

> *Happiness is the simplest form of gratitude.*
> *– Karl Barth*

Question #1: What went well today? Why? Find 3 pleasant experiences.

1. _____

_____

2. _____

_____

3. _____

_____

Question #2: Write about an event in the past that has given you joy. What happened? Where have you been? What exactly did you feel?

_____

_____

_____

_____

Question #3: What are you looking forward to tomorrow?

_____

Day 32

> *Humor is one of the best clothes you can wear*
> *in company. – William Shakespeare]*

Question #1: Where have I used my strengths today? Why? Name 3 things.

1. _____

   _____

2. _____

   _____

3. _____

   _____

Question #2: What was funny today? Why? Name three things.

1. _____

   _____

2. _____

   _____

3. _____

   _____

Question #3: What are you looking forward to tomorrow?

_____

Day 33

> The ability to live happily comes from a power
> inherent in the soul. – Marcus Aurelius

Question #1: What went well today? Why? Find 3 pleasant experiences.

1. _____

_____

2. _____

_____

3. _____

_____

Question #2: What didn't go the way you intended last week? Find the positive. What could be the lesson and the blessing?

_____

_____

_____

_____

_____

Question #3: What are you looking forward to tomorrow?

_____

Day 34

Date _____

Question #1: What went well today? Why? Find 3 pleasant experiences.

1. _____

   _____

2. _____

   _____

3. _____

   _____

Question #2: How could you give yourself a little joy every day? Find ideas.

_____

_____

_____

_____

_____

Question #3: What are you looking forward to tomorrow?

_____

Day 35

Date _____

> *Hardships prepare ordinary people for an extraordinary destiny.*
> *– C. S. Lewis*

Question #1: What was meaningful today? Why? Name three things.

1.
_____

_____

2.
_____

_____

3.
_____

_____

Question #2: What was funny today? Why? Name three things.

1.
_____

_____

2.
_____

_____

3.
_____

_____

Question #3: What are you looking forward to tomorrow?

_____

Day 36

> There it becomes bright in a human life, where
> one learns to praise and thank for the smallest
> things.– Friedrich von Bodelschwingh

Question #1: What went well today? Why? Find 3 pleasant experiences.

1.

2.

3.

Question #2: Write down 3-5 things you're grateful for.

1.

2.

3.

4.

5.

Question #3: What are you looking forward to tomorrow?

Day 37

> *Who knows his goal, finds the way.*
> *– Anonymous*

Question #1: Where have I used my strengths today? Why? Name 3 things.

1.

2.

3.

Question #2: Imagine a future for yourself in which everything went as you imagined it would. You have given your best, worked hard, and achieved all your goals. Now write down what you imagine.

Day 38

> *Not all storms come to shake you.*
> *Some come to clear your way. – Anonymous*

Question #1: What went well today? Why? Find 3 pleasant experiences.

1.

_____

2.

_____

3.

_____

_____

Question #2: Write about an event in the past that has given you joy. What happened? Where have you been? What exactly did you feel?

_____

_____

_____

_____

Question #3: What are you looking forward to tomorrow?

_____

Day 39

> *Every day you don't smile is a lost day.*
> *– Charlie Chaplin*

Question #1: Where have I used my strengths today? Why? Name 3 things.

1. _____

2. _____

3. _____

_____

Question #2: What was funny today? Why? Name three things.

1. _____

2. _____

3. _____

_____

Question #3: What are you looking forward to tomorrow?

_____

Day 40

> *Every new challenge is a gateway*
> *to new experiences. – Ernst Ferstl*

Question #1: What went well today? Why? Find 3 pleasant experiences.

1.
_____
_____
2.
_____
_____
3.
_____
_____

Question #2: What didn't go the way you intended last week? Find the positive. What could be the lesson and the blessing?

_____
_____
_____
_____
_____

Question #3: What are you looking forward to tomorrow?

_____

Day 41

> The smile you send returns to you.
> – Indian saying

Question #1: What went well today? Why? Find 3 pleasant experiences.

1. _____

   _____

2. _____

   _____

3. _____

   _____

Question #2: How could you give yourself a little joy every day? Find ideas.

_____

_____

_____

_____

_____

Question #3: What are you looking forward to tomorrow?

_____

Day 42

Date _____

> *Nothing in the world is as contagious as laughter and good mood.*
> *– Charles Dickens*

Question #1: What was meaningful today? Why? Name three things.

1.
_____

_____

2.
_____

_____

3.
_____

_____

Question #2: What was funny today? Why? Name three things.

1.
_____

_____

2.
_____

_____

3.
_____

_____

Question #3: What are you looking forward to tomorrow?

_____

Day 43

> *Thou shalt be grateful for the least, and thou*
> *shalt be worthy to receive greater things.*
> *– Thomas von Kempen*

Question #1: What went well today? Why? Find 3 pleasant experiences.

1. _____

_____

2. _____

_____

3. _____

_____

Question #2: Write down 3-5 things you're grateful for.

1. _____
2. _____
3. _____
4. _____
5. _____

Question #3: What are you looking forward to tomorrow?

_____

Day 44

> If you want to refresh yourself with the whole,
> then you must see the whole in the smallest.
> – Johann Wolfgang von Goethe

Question #1: Where have I used my strengths today? Why? Name 3 things.

1. _____

   _____

2. _____

   _____

3. _____

   _____

Question #2: Imagine a future for yourself in which everything went as you imagined it would. You have given your best, worked hard, and achieved all your goals. Now write down what you imagine.

_____

_____

_____

_____

_____

_____

Day 45

> We'll never know how much good a simple smile can do.
> – Mother Teresa

Question #1: What went well today? Why? Find 3 pleasant experiences.

1.
_____

_____

2.
_____

_____

3.
_____

_____

Question #2: Write about an event in the past that has given you joy. What happened? Where have you been? What exactly did you feel?

_____

_____

_____

_____

Question #3: What are you looking forward to tomorrow?

_____

Day 46

Date _____

> A life without joys is like a long journey without
> an inn. – Democritus

Question #1: Where have I used my strengths today?
Why? Name 3 things.

1. _____
_____

2. _____
_____

3. _____
_____

Question #2: What was funny today? Why? Name three
things.

1. _____
_____

2. _____
_____

3. _____
_____

Question #3: What are you looking forward to tomorrow?

_____

Day 47

> *Only the unpredictable turns the plan into a challenge. – Hans-Jürgen Quadbeck-Seeger*

Question #1: What went well today? Why? Find 3 pleasant experiences.

1. _____

_____

2. _____

_____

3. _____

_____

Question #2: What didn't go the way you intended last week? Find the positive. What could be the lesson and the blessing?

_____

_____

_____

_____

_____

Question #3: What are you looking forward to tomorrow?

_____

Day 48

> *The audience applauds fireworks,*
> *but no sunrise! – Friedrich Hebbel*

Question #1: What went well today? Why? Find 3 pleasant experiences.

1. _____

_____

2. _____

_____

3. _____

_____

Question #2: How could you give yourself a little joy every day? Find ideas.

_____

_____

_____

_____

_____

Question #3: What are you looking forward to tomorrow?

_____

Day 49

Date _____

Question #1: What was meaningful today? Why? Name three things.

1. _____

_____

2. _____

_____

3. _____

_____

Question #2: What was funny today? Why? Name three things.

1. _____

_____

2. _____

_____

3. _____

_____

Day 50

> *Gratitude is the first and the last feeling of a person. – Adolph Kolping*

Question #1: What went well today? Why? Find 3 pleasant experiences.

1.

_____

_____

2.

_____

_____

3.

_____

_____

Question #2: Write down 3-5 things you're grateful for.

1. _____

2. _____

3. _____

4. _____

5. _____

Question #3: What are you looking forward to tomorrow?

_____

Day 51

> It's not how much we have, it's how much we en-
> joy being happy. – Charles Spurgeon

Question #1: Where have I used my strengths today?
Why? Name 3 things.

1.
_____

_____

2.
_____

_____

3.
_____

_____

Question #2: Imagine a future for yourself in which everything went as you imagined it would. You have given
your best, worked hard, and achieved all your goals.
Now write down what you imagine.

_____

_____

_____

_____

_____

_____

Day 52

Date _____

Question #1: What went well today? Why? Find 3 pleasant experiences.

1.
_____

_____

2.
_____

_____

3.
_____

_____

Question #2: Write about an event in the past that has given you joy. What happened? Where have you been? What exactly did you feel?

_____

_____

_____

_____

Question #3: What are you looking forward to tomorrow?

_____

Day 53

Date _____

> Happiness is a journey, not a destination.
> – Ben Sweetland

Question #1: Where have I used my strengths today? Why? Name 3 things.

1. _____

2. _____

3. _____

_____

Question #2: What was funny today? Why? Name three things.

1. _____

2. _____

3. _____

_____

Question #3: What are you looking forward to tomorrow?

_____

Day 54

Date _____

> *Be happy -- you deserve it. – Anonymous*

Question #1: What went well today? Why? Find 3 pleasant experiences.

1. _____

_____

2. _____

_____

3. _____

_____

Question #2: What didn't go the way you intended last week? Find the positive. What could be the lesson and the blessing?

_____

_____

_____

_____

_____

Question #3: What are you looking forward to tomorrow?

_____

Day 55

Date _____

Question #1: What went well today? Why? Find 3
pleasant experiences.

1. _____

_____

2. _____

_____

3. _____

_____

Question #2: How could you give yourself a little joy
every day? Find ideas.

_____

_____

_____

_____

_____

Question #3: What are you looking forward to tomorrow?

_____

Day 56

> *The way to happiness is not to worry about anything that is beyond our control. – Epictetus*

Question #1: What was meaningful today? Why? Name three things.

1. _____

   _____

2. _____

   _____

3. _____

   _____

Question #2: What was funny today? Why? Name three things.

1. _____

   _____

2. _____

   _____

3. _____

   _____

Question #3: What are you looking forward to tomorrow?

_____

Day 57

> *The happiness of your life depends on the nature of your thoughts. – Marcus Aurelius*

Question #1: What went well today? Why? Find 3 pleasant experiences.

1. _____

_____

2. _____

_____

3. _____

_____

Question #2: Write down 3-5 things you're grateful for.

1. _____
2. _____
3. _____
4. _____
5. _____

Question #3: What are you looking forward to tomorrow?

_____

Day 58

> Do not give up, even if your suffering is too
> great; perhaps misfortune is the source of your
> happiness. – Menander

Question #1: Where have I used my strengths today?
Why? Name 3 things.

1. _____

_____

2. _____

_____

3. _____

_____

Question #2: Imagine a future for yourself in which everything went as you imagined it would. You have given
your best, worked hard, and achieved all your goals.
Now write down what you imagine.

_____

_____

_____

_____

_____

_____

Day 59

> There are many ways to happiness. One of them is to stop
> yammering. – Albert Einstein

Question #1: What went well today? Why? Find 3
pleasant experiences.

1. _____
_____

2. _____
_____

3. _____
_____

Question #2: Write about an event in the past that has
given you joy. What happened? Where have you been?
What exactly did you feel?

_____
_____
_____
_____

Question #3: What are you looking forward to tomorrow?

_____

Day 60

> *Most people are unhappy because they demand*
> *too much from happiness. Ambition is the*
> *greatest enemy of happiness because it blinds*
> *us. – Jean-Paul Belmondo*

Question #1: Where have I used my strengths today? Why? Name 3 things.

1. _____

_____

2. _____

_____

3. _____

_____

Question #2: What was funny today? Why? Name three things.

1. _____

_____

2. _____

_____

3. _____

_____

Day 61

> *The true art of living is to see the miraculous in everyday life. – Pearl S. Buck*

Question #1: What went well today? Why? Find 3 pleasant experiences.

1. _____

_____

2. _____

_____

3. _____

_____

Question #2: What didn't go the way you intended last week? Find the positive. What could be the lesson and the blessing?

_____

_____

_____

_____

_____

Question #3: What are you looking forward to tomorrow?

_____

Day 62

> The true artists of life are already happy if they
> are not unhappy. – Jean Anouilh

Question #1: What went well today? Why? Find 3 pleasant experiences.

1. _____

_____

2. _____

_____

3. _____

_____

Question #2: How could you give yourself a little joy every day? Find ideas.

_____

_____

_____

_____

_____

Question #3: What are you looking forward to tomorrow?

_____

Day 63

Date _____

> No one is perfect. Happiness means knowing your limits and love them. – Romain Rolland

Question #1: What was meaningful today? Why? Name three things.

1. _____

_____

2. _____

_____

3. _____

_____

Question #2: What was funny today? Why? Name three things.

1. _____

_____

2. _____

_____

3. _____

_____

Question #3: What are you looking forward to tomorrow?

_____

Day 64

> *Pay attention to the small in the world. That makes life richer and happier. – Carl Hilty*

Question #1: What went well today? Why? Find 3 pleasant experiences.

1. _____
_____

2. _____
_____

3. _____
_____

Question #2: Write down 3-5 things you're grateful for.

1. _____
2. _____
3. _____
4. _____
5. _____

Question #3: What are you looking forward to tomorrow?

_____

Day 65

> The secret of happiness lies not in possession,
> but in giving. Who makes others happy becomes
> happy. – André Gide

Question #1: Where have I used my strengths today?
Why? Name 3 things.

1. _____

_____

2. _____

_____

3. _____

_____

Question #2: Imagine a future for yourself in which everything went as you imagined it would. You have given
your best, worked hard, and achieved all your goals.
Now write down what you imagine.

_____

_____

_____

_____

_____

_____

Day 66

Date _____

Question #1: What went well today? Why? Find 3 pleasant experiences.

1. _____

   _____

2. _____

   _____

3. _____

   _____

Question #2: Write about an event in the past that has given you joy. What happened? Where have you been? What exactly did you feel?

_____

_____

_____

_____

Question #3: What are you looking forward to tomorrow?

_____

Day 67

Date _____

Question #1: Where have I used my strengths today?
Why? Name 3 things.

1. _____

_____

2. _____

_____

3. _____

_____

Question #2: What was funny today? Why? Name three
things.

1. _____

_____

2. _____

_____

3. _____

_____

Question #3: What are you looking forward to tomorrow?

_____

Day 68

Date _____

> Better less and satisfaction than much and
> quarrel and conflict. – Benjamin Franklin

Question #1: What went well today? Why? Find 3 pleasant experiences.

1. _____

_____

2. _____

_____

3. _____

_____

Question #2: What didn't go the way you intended last week? Find the positive. What could be the lesson and the blessing?

_____

_____

_____

_____

_____

Question #3: What are you looking forward to tomorrow?

_____

Day 69

> The beauty of things lives in the soul of the one
> who looks at them.– David Hume

Question #1: What went well today? Why? Find 3 pleasant experiences.

1.

_____

2.

_____

3.

_____

Question #2: How could you give yourself a little joy every day? Find ideas.

_____

_____

_____

_____

_____

Question #3: What are you looking forward to tomorrow?

_____

Day 70

> *Pleasure may be based on illusion, but happiness is based solely on truth. – Nicolas Chamfort*

Question #1: What was meaningful today? Why? Name three things.

1. _____

_____

2. _____

_____

3. _____

_____

Question #2: What was funny today? Why? Name three things.

1. _____

_____

2. _____

_____

3. _____

_____

Question #3: What are you looking forward to tomorrow?

_____

Day 71

> *A true friend contributes more to our happiness than a thousand enemies to our unhappiness. ~ Marie von Ebner-Eschenbach*

Question #1: What went well today? Why? Find 3 pleasant experiences.

1. _____

_____

2. _____

_____

3. _____

_____

Question #2: Write down 3-5 things you're grateful for.

1. _____
2. _____
3. _____
4. _____
5. _____

Question #3: What are you looking forward to tomorrow?

_____

Day 72

Date _____

> When you're happy, you shouldn't want to be
> happier. – Theodor Fontane

Question #1: Where have I used my strengths today?
Why? Name 3 things.

1.
_____

_____

2.
_____

_____

3.
_____

_____

Question #2: Imagine a future for yourself in which everything went as you imagined it would. You have given
your best, worked hard, and achieved all your goals.
Now write down what you imagine.

_____

_____

_____

_____

_____

_____

Day 73

> Happiness is the only thing that doubles when you share it.
> – Albert Schweitzer

Question #1: What went well today? Why? Find 3 pleasant experiences.

1. _____

2. _____

3. _____

_____

Question #2: Write about an event in the past that has given you joy. What happened? Where have you been? What exactly did you feel?

_____

_____

_____

_____

Question #3: What are you looking forward to tomorrow?

_____

Day 74

> *Almost everywhere, where there is happiness,*
> *there is joy in nonsense. – Friedrich Nietzsche*

Question #1: Where have I used my strengths today? Why? Name 3 things.

1. _____

_____

2. _____

_____

3. _____

_____

Question #2: What was funny today? Why? Name three things.

1. _____

_____

2. _____

_____

3. _____

_____

Question #3: What are you looking forward to tomorrow?

_____

Day 75

Date _____

> The door to happiness opens to the outside -
> those who try to "run it in" only close it.
> – Søren Kierkegaard

Question #1: What went well today? Why? Find 3 pleasant experiences.

1. _____

_____

2. _____

_____

3. _____

_____

Question #2: What didn't go the way you intended last week? Find the positive. What could be the lesson and the blessing?

_____

_____

_____

_____

_____

Question #3: What are you looking forward to tomorrow?

_____

Day 76

> Comparison is the end of happiness and the beginning of dissatisfaction. – Søren Kierkegaard

Question #1: What went well today? Why? Find 3 pleasant experiences.

1. _____

_____

2. _____

_____

3. _____

_____

Question #2: How could you give yourself a little joy every day? Find ideas.

_____

_____

_____

_____

_____

Question #3: What are you looking forward to tomorrow?

_____

Day 77

> *The highest pleasure is the satisfaction with oneself.*
> *– Jean-Jacques Rousseau*

Question #1: What was meaningful today? Why? Name three things.

1. _____

_____

2. _____

_____

3. _____

_____

Question #2: What was funny today? Why? Name three things.

1. _____

_____

2. _____

_____

3. _____

_____

Question #3: What are you looking forward to tomorrow?

_____

Day 78

> You don't just want to be happy, you
> want to be happier than the others. And
> this is so difficult because we think the
> others are happier than they are.
> – Charles-Louis de Montesquieu

Question #1: What went well today? Why? Find 3 pleasant experiences.

1.

2.

3.

Question #2: Write down 3-5 things you're grateful for.

1.

2.

3.

4.

5.

Question #3: What are you looking forward to tomorrow?

Day 79

> *Most people simply make themselves dissatis-*
> *fied by exaggerated demands on fate.*
> *– Wilhelm von Humboldt*

Question #1: Where have I used my strengths today?
Why? Name 3 things.

1. _____

   _____

2. _____

   _____

3. _____

   _____

Question #2: Imagine a future for yourself in which everything went as you imagined it would. You have given
your best, worked hard, and achieved all your goals.
Now write down what you imagine.

_____

_____

_____

_____

_____

_____

Day 80

> *It's little you need for blessedness.*
> *– Friedrich von Schiller*

Question #1: What went well today? Why? Find 3 pleasant experiences.

1. _____
   _____

2. _____
   _____

3. _____
   _____

Question #2: Write about an event in the past that has given you joy. What happened? Where have you been? What exactly did you feel?

_____

_____

_____

_____

Question #3: What are you looking forward to tomorrow?

_____

Day 81

> If in addition to a painless state comes the absence of boredom, then earthly happiness is essentially achieved. – Arthur Schopenhauer

Question #1: Where have I used my strengths today? Why? Name 3 things.

1.
_____

2.
_____

3.
_____

Question #2: What was funny today? Why? Name three things.

1.
_____

2.
_____

3.
_____

Question #3: What are you looking forward to tomorrow?

_____

Day 82

> *A moment of happiness outweighs thousands of*
> *years of posthumous rest.*
> *– Friedrich II. der Große*

Question #1: What went well today? Why? Find 3 pleasant experiences.

1. _____

_____

2. _____

_____

3. _____

_____

Question #2: What didn't go the way you intended last week? Find the positive. What could be the lesson and the blessing?

_____

_____

_____

_____

Question #3: What are you looking forward to tomorrow?

_____

Day 83

> Happiness does not live in possession and not
> in gold. Happiness is at home in the soul.
> – Democritus

Question #1: What went well today? Why? Find 3 pleasant experiences.

1. _____

   _____

2. _____

   _____

3. _____

   _____

Question #2: How could you give yourself a little joy every day? Find ideas.

_____

_____

_____

_____

_____

Question #3: What are you looking forward to tomorrow?

_____

Day 84

Date _____

> *Not who has little, but who desires much, is poor. – Seneca*

Question #1: What was meaningful today? Why? Name three things.

1.
_____

_____

2.
_____

_____

3.
_____

_____

Question #2: What was funny today? Why? Name three things.

1.
_____

_____

2.
_____

_____

3.
_____

_____

Question #3: What are you looking forward to tomorrow?

_____

Day 85

> Do not linger in the past, do not dream of the
> future. Concentrate on the present moment.
> – Buddha

Question #1: What went well today? Why? Find 3 pleasant experiences.

1. _____

_____

2. _____

_____

3. _____

_____

Question #2: Write down 3-5 things you're grateful for.

1. _____
2. _____
3. _____
4. _____
5. _____

Question #3: What are you looking forward to tomorrow?

_____

Day 86

Date _____

Question #1: Where have I used my strengths today? Why? Name 3 things.

1.
_____

_____

2.
_____

_____

3.
_____

_____

Question #2: Imagine a future for yourself in which everything went as you imagined it would. You have given your best, worked hard, and achieved all your goals. Now write down what you imagine.

_____

_____

_____

_____

_____

_____

Day 87

> Blessed can also be the one who, guided by reason, desires nothing more and fears nothing more. – Seneca

Question #1: What went well today? Why? Find 3 pleasant experiences.

1. _____

_____

2. _____

_____

3. _____

_____

Question #2: Write about an event in the past that has given you joy. What happened? Where have you been? What exactly did you feel?

_____

_____

_____

_____

Question #3: What are you looking forward to tomorrow?

_____

Day 88

> *Give up winning - and find happiness.*
> *– Buddha*

Question #1: Where have I used my strengths today? Why? Name 3 things.

1.

2.

3.

Question #2: What was funny today? Why? Name three things.

1.

2.

3.

Question #3: What are you looking forward to tomorrow?

Day 89

Date _____

> *Trust in your happiness - and you invite it.*
> *– Seneca*

Question #1: What went well today? Why? Find 3 pleasant experiences.

1. _____

_____

2. _____

_____

3. _____

_____

Question #2: What didn't go the way you intended last week? Find the positive. What could be the lesson and the blessing?

_____

_____

_____

_____

_____

Question #3: What are you looking forward to tomorrow?

_____

Day 90

> This world is in constant change. Growth and
> decay are its true nature. Things appear and
> dissolve again. Happy if one looks at them
> peacefully. – Buddha

Question #1: What went well today? Why? Find 3 pleasant experiences.

1. _____

_____

2. _____

_____

3. _____

_____

Question #2: How could you give yourself a little joy every day? Find ideas.

_____

_____

_____

_____

_____

Question #3: What are you looking forward to tomorrow?

_____

How happy are you now?

Time flies -- the 90 days are already over. What happens now? If you like, you can check whether you have really become happier.

1. In general, I consider myself...

| 1 | 2 | 3 | 4 | 5 | 6 | 7 |

not a very
happy person

a very
happy person

2. Compared with the most of my peers, I consider myself...

| 1 | 2 | 3 | 4 | 5 | 6 | 7 |

less happy

more happy

3. Some people are generally very happy. They enjoy life regardless of what is going on, getting the most out of everything. To what extent does this characterization describe you?

| 1 | 2 | 3 | 4 | 5 | 6 | 7 |

not at all

a great deal

4. Some people are generally not very happy. Although they are not depressed, they never seem as happy as they might be. To what extent does this characterization describe you?

| 1 | 2 | 3 | 4 | 5 | 6 | 7 |

a great deal

not at all

Make a circle around the value that applies to you. Then calculate your average value. The resulting value is your current happiness level.

Compare it with your happiness level 90 days ago. By the way, you can also increase my happiness level by sending me your happiness values before and after keeping the diary:

detlef@detlefbeeker.de

I'm glad the happiness journal helped you.

What's the next step?

If you're happier, I suggest you keep the diary. It has already become a habit anyway, so it should be easy for you now. Just write down the questions and answer them. You can also download the templates from my website for seven days and print them out.

Day 1

Date _____

> *Our true purpose is to be happy. — Dalai Lama*

Question #1: What went well today? Why? Find 3 pleasant experiences.

1. _____

2. _____

3. _____

Question #2: Write down 3-5 things you're grateful for.

1. _____
2. _____
3. _____
4. _____
5. _____

Question #3: What are you looking forward to tomorrow?

_____

~ 18 ~

You can find the templates below:

http://www.detlefbeeker.de/ happiness-templates

The important thing is that you keep doing it in writing. You can keep the diary on your PC or, even better, in a nice booklet.

I hope you enjoyed the journal.

Warm regards,

Detlef Beeker

Made in the USA
Middletown, DE
31 August 2020

16988321R00068